BORN TO BE A
WARRIOR

Your Governmental Authority in Christ

Angela Brown

Cover Design: Sarah Delaney

Book Editing: Angela Brown

Book Layout © 2014 BookesignTemplates.com

Dedication

Dedicated to all the brave warriors in God's army that have gone on before me and come along beside me to teach, train, and encourage me to use the awesome authority Christ has freely given to me as His born-again creation.

Table of Contents

INTRODUCTION

Recently, I have been praying about what the Lord would want me to write next. I finished a year-long devotional book last year and have been resting from writing. But I knew in my spirit that I had more books to come.

A few days ago, I woke from a dream in which I was instructed to write about the armor of God that the Lord gives each of His followers. It is described in the Book of Ephesians, Chapter Six.

I have researched and recorded what the Lord has shared with me through study and practice about the armor He has prepared for us to wear and the victories He has for us to win. I know this is just an introduction to the depths of understanding we can learn about being a warrior in God's army.

I pray that the following scriptures and revelations will be an encouragement to you to take your place in the army of the Living God and fulfill your call to be a warrior for the Kingdom of God on Earth.

Remember that the words you speak and the actions you take in your life will affect the generations that follow you. Be strong and courageous and make a way for those that come behind you to discover and know the Lord God intimately and glorify Him as His children.

Enjoy your journey in learning how to be the mighty warrior He created you to be.

Angela Brown
May/2022

CHAPTER 1
God, the Author of Authority

*God said, Let Us [Father, Son, and Holy Spirit] make
mankind in Our image, after Our likeness, and let them
have complete authority over the fish of the sea, the birds
of the air, the [tame]
beasts, and over all of the earth, and over everything that
creeps upon the earth.
So God created man in His own image, in the image and
likeness of God He created him; male and female He
created them.
And God blessed them and said to them, Be fruitful,
multiply, and fill the earth, and subdue it [using all its vast
resources in the service of God and man]; and have
dominion over the fish of the sea, the birds of the air, and
over every living creature that moves upon the earth.*
Genesis 1:26-28 The Amplified Bible

The Lord God Almighty created men and women in His own image. We are to rule and reign over the resources and creatures of the Earth as God desires. God created mankind to walk in *dominion* on Earth. We are to be those who use the resources He has provided for His service and the good of all His creation. We are created to have authority in the maintenance and protection of God's creation.

That word, *dominion,* in the original Hebrew text, means *to prevail against, reign, (bear, make to) rule, (over), take.* As those created in God's image, we are to prevail against any force that would use the Earth, its resources, and its people in ways that would not be in God's will. We are to rule and reign over what God has given us on Earth as He would. We are to take the resources God has provided on Earth and use them for His glory.

As God's representatives, we must bear the responsibility to walk and live on the Earth as He created us to. He has provided us access to many resources and much power through our relationship with Father, Son, and Holy Spirit. Christ Jesus is our example of the supreme authority exercised on Earth.

[The Father] has delivered and drawn us to Himself out of the control and the dominion of darkness and has transferred us into the kingdom of the Son of His love,
In Whom we have our redemption through His blood, [which means] the forgiveness of our sins. [Now] He is the exact likeness of the unseen God [the visible representation of the invisible];
He is the Firstborn of all creation.
For it was in Him that all things were created, in heaven and on earth, things seen and things unseen, whether thrones, dominions, rulers, or authorities; all things were created and exist through Him [by His service, intervention] and in and for Him.
And He Himself existed before all things, and in Him all things consist (cohere, are held together).
Colossians 1:13-17 The Amplified Bible

Jesus co-created all authority along with Father God. Jesus always walked in the authority of Father God when He walked on Earth. He followed the Father's lead in exercising kingdom authority throughout His life. He submitted to the Father's desires even when His flesh was resisting the responsibility. He was persecuted and demeaned in ways most of us have never experienced. But

He was always walking in the authority given to Him to be the Savior of the world.

> *For even as the Father has life in Himself and is self-existent,*
> *so He has given to the Son to have life in Himself and be self-existent.*
> *And He has given Him authority and granted Him power to execute (exercise, practice)*
> *judgment because He is a Son of man [very man].*
> John 5:26-27 The Amplified Bible

Every Christian is to be an example of Christ's authority. Every day presents opportunities to stand strong on our faith in the Lord and reflect His grace and power through our lives. We are part of God's kingdom army on Earth. We are created to be victorious warriors that walk in truth and authority from Father, Son, and Holy Spirit.

As any warrior must do, we train and learn how to wield this power and authority wisely. We are also required to learn how to use the resources He gives us for His glory, our good, and the benefit of others. We are created to be warriors in God's army to protect and preserve lives and the resources He gives us.

CHAPTER 2
Who is the Enemy?

If we are created to be warriors in God's army, then who is the enemy we are expected to encounter and subdue? Isn't God the supreme authority? Why does He need an army? Father God has given every person the ability to **choose** to follow Him and recognize Jesus Christ as their Lord and Savior. He doesn't demand our loyalty— He pursues us in love and grace. As followers of Christ, we are to surrender our agendas and follow His. We must choose His way above our own way.

God's desire is to win the hearts of every man, woman, and child so that they can benefit from being members of His family. As members of His family, we are also warriors, just like our brother Jesus. And we have an enemy who desires to draw us away from God's love and grace and hold us captive by his evil lies. That enemy is satan (the devil) and he has an army of demons that do his bidding.

Be well balanced and always alert, because your enemy,
the devil, roams around incessantly,
like a roaring lion looking for its prey to devour.
Take a decisive stand against him and resist his every
attack with strong, vigorous faith.
For you know that your believing brothers and sisters
around the world are experiencing the same kinds of
troubles you endure.
1 Peter 5:8-9 The Passion Translation

Every person on Earth is vulnerable to the attacks of the enemy. He uses thoughts, emotions, memories, sickness, and other people we may encounter to discourage us and keep us from becoming the people we were created to be. We may never see the devil or one of his demons, but we will all certainly experience their dark influence at some point in our lives.

BUT PRAISE THE LORD, the devil is a defeated foe! Jesus defeated his strategies on the cross and went to the pit of hell to defeat him in his own domain. And Jesus arose victorious carrying all who believe in Him into the place of victory.

For the Lord God is one, and so are we! For we share in one faith, one baptism, and one Father. He is the perfect Father who leads us all, works through us all, and lives in us all! And he has generously given each one of us supernatural grace,
according to the size of the gift of Christ.
This is why he says:
"He ascends into the heavenly heights
Taking his many captured ones with him,
Leading them in triumphal procession,
And gifts were given to men."
Having first descended into hell, he has ascended triumphantly into the heights of heaven to begin the restoration and fulfillment of all things.
Ephesians 4:5-10 The Passion Translation

Our God's desire is that every follower of Christ Jesus will lead a victorious life by defeating every plot and plan of the enemy of their souls through their faith in His work on the cross. As a child of God and follower of Christ, you have a part to play in the *restoration and fulfillment of all things.*

You are destined for victory and can experience that victory on Earth as you follow the lead of Holy Spirit to exemplify the life of Christ through your words and actions. The enemy is defeated but continues to harass every person on Earth to keep them from experiencing the victorious power of Jesus Christ, our Savior, and Lord.

Father God has created you to reflect the **glory and power** of Jesus Christ as you grow and mature in your faith. Every phase of life presents new opportunities to show others the goodness and greatness of our Creator, Savior, and Counselor. We will always be expanding in victory if we follow the voice of the Father, Son, and Holy Spirit. Studying His written word and learning to hear His voice in our spirit are vital tools to keep moving forward in victory.

God has also provided armor for His warriors. We must learn how to wear it effectively for our protection against the enemy of our souls—the devil. He has given us weapons to use to defeat the enemy and maintain peace and provision for our lives, our loved ones, and our countries.

For though we walk (live) in the flesh, we are not carrying on our warfare according to the flesh and using mere human weapons.
For the weapons of our warfare are not physical [weapons of flesh and blood], but they are mighty before God for the overthrow and destruction of strongholds,
[Inasmuch as we] refute arguments and theories and reasonings and every proud and lofty thing that sets itself up against the [true] knowledge of God; and we lead every thought and purpose away captive into the obedience of Christ (the Messiah, the Anointed One),
2 Corinthians 10:3-5 The Amplified Bible

As children of the Living God and members of His army, we fight in a spiritual war. Therefore, we must be equipped with spiritual weapons and spiritual armor. Whether we ever become a part of a physical army on Earth or not, we must be equipped to stand against our greatest enemy—the devil. This spiritual armor and weaponry are a must for every believer in Christ Jesus. We cannot become all God has created us to be or accomplish all He created us to accomplish without being equipped with His armor and weapons and learning how to use them effectively.

This training for warfare begins with the renewing of our minds. We cannot think like the world thinks or respond as those with no hope or wisdom. Our thoughts must come into alignment with the thoughts of our Father, His Son, and the Holy Spirit. We were created in Their image so we must learn to think as They do and act as They lead us to act. The *true knowledge of God* is key to becoming the mighty warriors He created us to be.

Assuming that you have really heard Him and been taught by Him, as [all] Truth is in Jesus [embodied and personified in Him],
Strip yourselves of your former nature [put off and discard your old unrenewed self] which characterized your previous manner of life and becomes corrupt through lusts and desires that spring from delusion;
And be constantly renewed in the spirit of your mind [having a fresh mental and spiritual attitude],
And put on the new nature (the regenerate self) created in God's image, [Godlike] in true righteousness and holiness.
Ephesians 4:21-24 The Amplified Bible

The process of renewing our minds takes time and patience. We must purpose to put ourselves in places and with people who will aid us in discovering the true knowledge of the Father, Son, and Spirit. As we learn of the Godhead and Their love, mercy, grace, and power, we can then step into the true identity of whom They created us to be. We must surrender to the will of God and not our own selfish desires. What we knew of ourselves and others before we met Jesus as Savior and King will change when we learn of God's ways and desires. He is patient beyond our imaginations, but we must purpose in our hearts to learn of Him and His wisdom so we can become equipped and prepared to fight the spiritual war that is before every believer.

By studying God's word about the armor and weapons He has provided, we learn how to use them wisely with the help and leadership of the Holy Spirit. Holy Spirit is our counselor and the one who reminds us of what Jesus taught and projected when He walked on Earth. Holy Spirit is our help mate and comforting companion as we train and learn Father God's ways. Jesus, Himself, gave us this wonderful promise:

If you [really] love Me, you will keep (obey) My commands.
And I will ask the Father, and He will give you another
Comforter (Counselor, Helper, Intercessor, Advocate,
Strengthener, and Standby), that He may remain with you
forever—
The Spirit of Truth, Whom the world cannot receive
(welcome, take to its heart) because it does not see Him or
know and recognize Him. But you know and recognize Him,
for He lives with you [constantly] and will be in you.
John 14:15-17 The Amplified Bible

So, be assured as you study the Word of God concerning the spiritual armor and weaponry, He has provided for you, Holy Spirit will be present to counsel and advise you on how to use it properly for the glory of God and for your own benefit. It is a study well worth your time and energy. The understanding you gain will take you farther and higher into the glorious plan the Lord has for your life.

CHAPTER 3
Your Need for Armor

The Book of Ephesians in the New Testament Bible was written by the Apostle Paul. He wrote many letters of encouragement and wisdom to those who believed that Jesus was the Son of God. These letters contained much teaching and revelation about whom God created His people to be as they followed His lead and put their faith in His love and wisdom.

In Chapter Six of Ephesians, Paul talks about the armor of God that every believer should be wearing. He knew that there would be many challenges ahead for those who wanted to follow God in the world we live in. The world is full of hard people, difficult situations, and scary places that every person will eventually encounter. So, our loving Father in Heaven designed special armor for us to wear as we go about our lives in this challenging world. Paul describes the armor and how to use it as we walk through life so that we can be victorious children of God.

In verses 10-13 of Ephesians 6, Paul begins to explain the reason we need to be clothed in the armor of God:

In conclusion, be strong in the Lord [be empowered through your union with Him]; draw your strength from Him [that strength which His boundless might provide]. Put on God's whole armor [the armor of a heavy-armed soldier which God supplies], that you may be able successfully to stand up against [all] the strategies and the deceits of the devil.
For we are not wrestling with flesh and blood [contending only with physical opponents], but against the despotisms,

*against the powers, against [the master spirits who are]
the world rulers of this present darkness, against the spirit
forces of wickedness in the heavenly
(supernatural) sphere.
Therefore put on God's complete armor, that you may be
able to resist and stand your ground on the evil day [of
danger], and, having done all [the crisis demands],
to stand [firmly in your place].*
The Amplified Bible

As you can see in these verses, we face an enemy that cannot be seen with our physical eyes. He is the devil. He uses wicked schemes and evil lies to cause us to be afraid and deny that Jesus is Lord and that God is our Father. They are greater than the devil. We must continually draw our strength from the Lord who created us to be strong and successful warriors.

The devil has already lost the war, but he wants us to think that we cannot win the battles we face in the world to become all God created us to be. As we **focus on the Lord and not the devil,** Father God strengthens us through His written word and encourages our spirits to rise and move forward to become mighty sons and daughters of the Living God.

Your personal relationship with the Father, Son, and Holy Spirit is the platform that enables you to gain Their supernatural strength, truth, and wisdom and use it for the glory of God and the benefit of others and yourself. You cannot remain strong against the powers of the enemy without the power of the Living God working in you and through you. Your union with God is vital to make you complete and empower you to defeat the enemy and project the goodness and greatness of the Lord through your life. You must have an honest and intimate union with Father, Son, and Holy Spirit. They are your power source. The Passion Translation of verse 11 offers a very interesting fact:

Put on the full suit of armor that God wears when he goes into battle,
so that you will be protected as you fight against the evil strategies of the accuser!

Did you hear that? God wears armor to go into battle! Jesus wore that armor as He walked the Earth and confronted many enemies, both physical and spiritual. So if God Himself wears armor, then we too, need to put on His armor for our protection as we live out life on Earth.

Our enemy, the devil, has many ways to defeat us in life. He projects thoughts that cause worry, fear, anxiety, hatred, hopelessness, shame, pride, and many other negative feelings to keep us powerless and weak.

Paul explains that the enemy is not flesh and blood, a physical opponent, but a spiritual one. He can and does use people to oppose us. Paul uses the word *despotism* to describe this facet of the enemy. According to Webster's dictionary, despotism is *a system of government in which the ruler has unlimited power.*

The devil has unlimited power on Earth except in the lives of people who have chosen Jesus to be their Savior and Lord. The blood of Jesus on the cross washes us clean and ushers us into the Kingdom of God where the devil has no authority. When you are saved and walk in obedience to the Lord, you are no longer living according to the government of the enemy. Now you walk according to the government of God. The Lord gives His saved ones power and authority over the devil and all his demons. God's people can supersede the devil's plots and plans by obeying the government of the Lord and speaking His living word over their lives.

The devil no longer has absolute power on Earth because the people who are saved and delivered through Jesus have the power of the Kingdom of God backing their pure lives and words. So, as you walk in the saving grace of Jesus Christ, you become an overcoming force against the despotism of the devil!

As you begin to walk in the power of the Kingdom of God, He will teach and direct you to pray, speak and act according to His government and no longer under the government of the enemy. As you do that, you will be able to suppress and overcome every evil spirit power of darkness that you encounter in your life on Earth. You will operate with the power from God, your Creator, and you will defy and overcome the influence of the powers and world rulers of darkness and spirit forces of wickedness that have operated so freely in the world.

God's armor is your protection and instrument of power to overcome the evil enemy of your spirit, soul, and body. God has freely provided this armor for you and equipped you as a powerful soldier in His army on Earth. The resurrection power of Christ is appropriated to you as you walk in obedience to His written and personal words of instruction and correction. Thus, your union and intimacy with the Lord become the power source you need to overcome every plot and plan of the devil against your life. You were created to be a victorious warrior and child of the Living God of the universe!

Just like any soldier, you need to learn how to use the armor God has provided to become a successful, mighty warrior in the His kingdom. As you grow more knowledgeable in the Word of God and remain faithful to His leadership, your authority on Earth will increase. The

Father desires for you to continue to grow in faith and power all the days of your life. Expect His power to increase as you mature in your relationship with Him. He desires to raise you up as a pure and powerful reflection of His loving kindness and authority in your realms of influence. Always expect an increase from the Lord in every area of your life.

Remember intimacy with God is developed by spending time with Him and in His written Word. Time spent in worship and prayer and study of God's Word is a key factor in becoming a victorious child of God. He is faithful to His faithful children.

CHAPTER 4
Your Armor Revealed

Every warrior going into battle must be adequately clothed and equipped to face their enemy with protective armor and powerful weapons. A warrior must also remember whom they are representing as they fight the enemy.

Clothe yourselves therefore, as God's own chosen ones (His own picked representatives),
[who are] purified and holy and well-loved [by God Himself...
Colossians 3:12a The Amplified Bible

Remember that you are God's chosen representative on Earth as you face opposition from the enemy of your soul. God loves you and wants you to be fully clothed in the mighty armor that He provides for His soldiers. You are fighting for the righteousness of God to prevail on Earth. Therefore, you need to be clothed in His righteous ways to be successful on the battlefield.

Father God is always ready and excited to teach His children more of His powerful ways to reflect His glory and defeat the enemy of His family. He never tires of training and strengthening His loved ones. Open your heart to receive all He has for you!

Now we will begin to examine God's **complete** armor. You need every single piece of the armor He provides to be the strong warrior He created you to be. And after you are fully clothed in that armor, you will need to learn how to stand firm in the place He calls you to be so that you can resist and overcome the plots of the enemy.

BELT OF TRUTH

Stand therefore [hold your ground], having tightened the belt of truth around your loins...
Ephesians 6:13-14a The Amplified Bible

The first piece of armor Paul mentions is the **belt of truth**. I think it is interesting that he starts with the belt. A belt is the thing that we use to hold up our pants. You definitely need your pants on to face the enemy!

The belt is positioned in the middle of your body. It supports your clothing and secures it around your body. It surrounds your loins which is the reproductive part of your body. You are called to reproduce the likeness of Christ in your life. If you don't know God's truth about yourself and your enemy, then you cannot be all He has called you to be.

So, really, it is not so funny to be caught with your pants down! You need God's truth to be actively at work in your spirit, soul, and body. You need to be familiar with His written word and you need to be able to hear His voice speak the truth to you about your identity, your circumstances, and the enemy you face on a daily basis.

God's truth is the first piece of protection you must have in place. Without His wisdom and truth to guide you, you will certainly be uncovered and vulnerable in the battle against the enemy of lies. Truth is vital to becoming and maintaining a victorious warrior lifestyle. God's truth is your road map to victory. Clothe yourself daily in His words—written and spoken!

I believe that the primary element of truth we must all take in is the fact that our Father in heaven has created us to have an active and intimate relationship with Him, the Lord Jesus Christ, and the Holy Spirit. Constant communication with the Living God of all creation is our life source. He has many facets and wants us to be familiar with them all. It takes time and patience to learn of Him and from Him. He enjoys our company and longs to share Himself with us as we come with open minds and hearts to receive His love, wisdom, correction, and guidance every day of our lives.

His truth only comes to us through His grace and mercy which is generously poured out to those who approach Him in humility and respect. He loves to fellowship with His children and teach us His loving and mighty ways to become all we were created to be. His truth is worth our sacrifice of time and energy. Without it, we will perish. His belt of truth is our first and foremost piece of armor.

By wearing the belt of truth, you can reap the blessing God created you to receive as we see in Genesis 1:28:

And God blessed them and said to them, Be fruitful, multiply, and fill the earth, and subdue it [using all its vast resources in the service of God and man]; and have dominion over the fish of the sea, the birds of the air, and over every living creature that moves upon the earth.

We cannot fulfill that role if we are not inspired and directed by His truth about how our lives should be managed.

We must be taught and trained with His truth so we can exercise the authority He has given us to influence and manage the territory we live in. We cannot let our selfish desires take precedence over His desire for our lives. So, we must wear the belt of truth to **be fruitful, multiply and fill the earth and subdue it!**

BREASTPLATE OF HOLINESSS

...and having put on the breastplate of integrity and of moral rectitude
and right standing with God...
Ephesians 6:14b The Amplified Bible

The next piece of armor we need to put on is the breastplate. The breastplate covers your heart, lungs and other vital organs that keep you alive. We can certainly see why you would need a breastplate in the heat of war. Even our modern-day police forces usually wear bullet proof vests over their chests for protection against dangerous criminals. If your heart or lungs are damaged, your life is certainly at risk. So, the breastplate is very important.

The Passion Translation of this verse says:

Put on holiness as the protective armor that covers your heart.

Most Christians don't believe they can become holy. That word seems to only fit God as our Father, Savior, and Holy Spirit. But when you look back at the Amplified Bible version of holiness, it defines it as *integrity, moral rectitude and right standing with God.*

If a person has surrendered their life to Jesus as their Savior and Lord, then they are covered and cleansed by the blood of the Lamb. They are not a sinner by nature anymore. They are considered a child of the Living God, therefore, holy by nature. Yes, they may occasionally commit a sin, but the conviction of the Lord will draw them back on the right path and they will walk in the holiness of God's nature through repentance and obedience.

Our wise and loving Father God knew we could not live a holy life without assistance. Thus, Jesus was sent to die for our sins and be resurrected to the right hand of His Father. And that is what happens to us as we give our lives to Him and confess Jesus as our Lord and Savior. Our Almighty God has made every provision for us to become and remain holy in His presence. By surrendering to His will and direction for our lives, we are putting on the breastplate that covers and protects our hearts from the evil ambushes of our enemy, the devil.

Obedience to God's truth forms that mighty breastplate around your heart. God's truth gives you the ability to change the unrighteous thoughts and attitudes that are embedded in your heart. Then, as you continue in obedience to His truth, your heart becomes stronger and more durable under the pressures of relationships and circumstances that you deal with in your daily life.

God's truth leads you to righteous obedience in word and in deed. Then, your heart is guarded against the lies of your enemy, the devil. With truth in place, your heart is able to beat like the Father's heart and motivate you to speak and act in holiness.

The breastplate guards the breath of your lungs from being used to speak defeat or death over your life or the lives of others. Your words carry great power and can create an atmosphere that can be used by the Lord or the devil. So, the breastplate of holiness is also vital in your ability to cleanse the atmosphere around you with your spoken words.

Praise God for the breastplate of holiness that He makes available to all His surrendered, obedient children. We all need it to be in place every day!

SHOES OF PEACE

And having shod your feet in preparation [to face the enemy with the firm-footed stability, the promptness, and the readiness produced by the good news] of the Gospel of peace.
Ephesians 6:15 The Amplified Bible

When I think of a soldier going into battle, I think of their heavy, supportive boots that are laced up above the ankles. They indeed give the warrior stability as they move about on the battlefield. These boots prepare them for uneven ground and protect them from being damaged by debris or traps lying in their pathway. It takes effort to put on these strong boots and they must be laced up properly to give the warrior the stability he will need to navigate the battlefield.

In Verse 15 of Ephesians 6, we see that this kind of preparation for the spiritual warrior is produced by receiving and believing the *good news of the Gospel of peace.* Understanding and accepting the peace that Jesus came to give you as your Savior and Lord is the preparation you must have to walk in stability throughout your life.

The circumstances in the world change daily. We live in an unstable environment. Peace in the world is temporary. Peace in the Kingdom of God is everlasting. God's peace does not change because your circumstances change. He is always available to give you the peace you need to walk in stability and readiness as you face changing circumstances. His peace enables you to move about on the battlefield of life without wavering and doubting and fearing the outcome of change and challenge.

Studying the Word of God and spending time in prayer before Him enables us to appropriate His peace in preparation for our battles. It takes time and effort to study and meditate and receive His Gospel of peace as our footwear for the battles we may face in life. As we learn and accept God's word as our guide and preparation for living life victoriously, we are ready for any challenge that we may encounter. We may not see the challenge in advance, but our strong shoes of peace keep us prepared to face and overcome the effects of the battles we may face.

Without God's peace present with us, it is hard to know what direction to walk in. When we don't have peace about what we are doing or where we are going, we need to stop and wait and listen for God's direction. The lack of peace can mean we are walking in the wrong direction, or we have not taken time to prepare ourselves with His wisdom for the task ahead.

Waiting on God can be very challenging. We tend to run out into busyness without stepping back in rest to gain the strength and preparation we need from Him to accomplish what He is calling us to do. Just as this verse from Ephesians instructs us, we need to take time to prepare ourselves with His peace so we can walk ahead on the right path. Even if that path contains multiple challenges, we can move with great stability and efficiency when His peace is present to assure us of His grace and support.

I also think of shoes as being the accent of any kind of clothing I put on. I don't wear high heels if I am going hiking. Shoes are the groundwork for our activity. So, the Gospel of peace is the groundwork for our daily walk with the Lord. His peace enables us to accomplish the tasks that we must carry out each day. Peace forms a platform for us to stand on and project the power and presence of our God on Earth. Walking in His peace gives us power and gives Him glory. You can't beat that kind of footwear!

SHIELD OF FAITH

Lift up over all the [covering] shield of saving faith, upon which you can quench all the flaming missiles of the wicked [one].
Ephesians 6:16 The Amplified Bible

During the time that Paul wrote these words, warriors carried large shields into battle. Each soldier had his own shield to cover the vulnerable parts of his body to further protect himself from the arrows of the enemy. These shields were door shaped and quite heavy. The warriors had to be strong just to carry them into battle.

Paul is portraying a Christian's shield to be one of *faith.* The Strong's Concordance describes faith as persuasion or conviction, especially reliance upon Christ for salvation. It also describes faith as assurance, belief, and fidelity.

As we progress through the trials and challenges of life, our faith in God and His goodness becomes our shield of protection. If we are persuaded that Christ is our Lord and Savior and are convicted of our need for Him in our lives, then we have faith. If we believe His love, grace, and mercy are available to direct our lives then we can move forward with faith. With faith in Christ, we become faithful to Him and remain loyal in our relationship with Him. Our faith in Christ as Savior and Lord keeps us assured of His ability to protect and defend us as we walk in obedience to His Word.

When I looked up the meaning of **shield** in this verse, I was so encouraged by what I found. The Greek word for shield means a door-shaped shield. But the root word for shield means *a portal or entrance,* hence, a gate. As we walk in faithful obedience to the Lord, we are entering a spiritual portal that takes us higher into His presence and power to accomplish our destiny as His children.

Wow, that is truly encouraging to think about as we continue to walk in His ways on Earth. Our faith in the Lord opens the gate for us to walk in Kingdom authority as we meet the enemy in battle. Thank You Lord, for giving us Your shield of faith!!

*The princes and nobles of the peoples are gathered together, a [united] people for the God of Abraham, **for the shields of the earth belong to God**; He is highly exalted.*
Psalm 47:9 The Amplified Bible
(The emphasis on shields is mine)

Notice in the above scripture that the shields belong to God. He has gifted us with these shields of faith. We don't buy them or manufacture them; they are pure gifts from God. He gives us His faith to accomplish our destiny and defeat the enemy of our souls. That is the reason for the high praise and worship of our generous and loving Father God.

Sing and celebrate! Sing some more, celebrate some more! Sing your highest song of praise to our King! For God is the Triumphant King; the powers of earth are all his. So sing your celebration songs of highest praise to the Glorious Enlightened One!

Our God reigns over every nation! He reigns on his holy throne over all.
All the nobles and princes, the loving servants of the God of Abraham, they all gather to worship. Every warrior's shield is now lowered as surrendered trophies before this King. He has taken his throne, high and lofty exalted over all!
Psalm 47:6-9 The Passion Translation

These verses from Psalm 47 are a great encouragement and powerful declarations for us to meditate on and pronounce out loud before the Lord. We must always take time to sing His praises and acknowledge His mighty reigning power over every nation. Notice in verse 9 that:

Every warrior's shield is now lowered as surrendered trophies before this King.

As warriors in God's army on Earth, we must lower our shields of faith before the Lord, our King, as a gift to Him. When we surrender our will to God and follow His ways instead of our own will, the faith we walk in becomes a trophy of the Lord's faithfulness. When we trust Him to provide protection and power as we face our enemy and accomplish our God-given destiny as His children, we honor Him as King and as our ultimate authority. His gift of faith to us is well worth our time to celebrate and thank Him for it.

I am also encouraged that this shield of faith *can quench **all** the flaming missiles of the wicked one.* Not one missile from the enemy of our souls can penetrate this shield of faith. It is completely strong and durable for all the battles we might face in life. Faith in the Lord is our ultimate defense against worry, doubt, fear, sickness, weakness, and lack of any kind. Christ strengthens and protects us as we walk through the portal of faith.

Faith in Christ is the doorway into the Kingdom of God and is always opened by trusting His words, example, and direction. Faith is not a one-time experience. We need faith for every part of our journey on Earth. Every day brings new experiences for us to exercise our faith in the Lord and enter His protection, power, and purposes for our lives. Some of our activities may look insignificant and not important enough for the exercise of faith. But I believe we need faith in the Lord just to get up every day and thank Him for providing the necessities of life.

My need for faith may look small compared to yours, but the Lord is ready to give us His protection and encouragement for even the smallest of tasks. Don't ever think your need is unimportant to Him. But realize He desires for you to grow in faith and pursue the higher purposes He has designed for you at every phase of your life. No matter your age or station in life, God will meet you and provide that open door for you to walk into His protection and power. Faith in Christ is the portal into His holy, protective presence!

HELMET OF SALVATION

And take the helmet of salvation...
Ephesians 6:17a

Helmets are a must for all who engage in warfare. The helmet protects the head of the warrior. Of course, the brain is in your head and is absolutely necessary to sustain the rest of your body. Your brain not only enables you to think, but it also sends signals to the other parts of your body so that the organs and tissues function properly. Without a helmet in warfare, the warrior is vulnerable to life-threatening trauma.

We know now that protecting the brain is so important that we are encouraged and sometimes, by law, forced to wear helmets. People who ride motorcycles and bikes need helmets. That would include children. People who climb mountains also wear helmets. Football players and snow skiers wear helmets. So, helmets are vital armor even while enjoying hobbies and sports.

When a person is traumatized by a blow to the brain, they suffer many different symptoms. It can cause loss of memory, loss of speech, loss of movement, loss of understanding simple words or instructions—loss of life. The list of losses is a long and daunting one. So, it is vital that we always protect our heads. That way our thinking processes are uninterrupted and healthy life is preserved.

So, in the context of spiritual warfare, you need a spiritual helmet to protect your brain from the effects of injury and trauma caused by the enemy of your soul—the devil. His plan is to invade your thinking and cause you to believe lies about yourself, your circumstances, God, or other people. If you continue to engage these evil thoughts on a regular basis, you can become traumatized and lose a healthy perspective on life. And those evil thoughts can even affect your physical health as well.

Protecting your mind is key in spiritual warfare. You must stay focused on the One who can change your unhealthy perspectives of life. Remaining focused on Father, Son, and Holy Spirit can guard your mind like a helmet guards your brain on the battlefield.

In this verse concerning the helmet of salvation, the Greek word for salvation is translated as a ***defense.*** Salvation through belief in Christ Jesus as your Lord and

Savior is your greatest defense against traumatic thinking. As you grow in knowledge and relationship with God, your thinking changes for the better. Unhealthy and evil thoughts are overcome by focusing on His words concerning who you are and who He is.

If you have put on the belt of truth by studying God's written word and learning to hear His spoken voice to you, you have begun the process of renewing your mind which forms the helmet of salvation. When you believe the truth that God speaks and apply it to your life, you have the defense you need against the onslaughts of the enemy of your soul.

Remember, as you go about your everyday routines or even fun activities that don't seem to be warlike, the enemy can attack your mind and bring great distress and distraction. **Salvation** is your strongest defense against the evil intrusions the enemy wants to make into your life. If your mind is protected by Christ's presence in your life, then you are free to go anywhere He may lead you with confidence and assurance that He will defend you.

Earlier in this letter that Paul wrote to the Ephesians, I believe he aptly describes what it means to put on the *helmet of salvation:*

Assuming that you have really heard Him and been taught by Him, as [all] Truth is in Jesus [embodied and personified in Him],
Strip yourselves of your former nature [put off and discard your old unrenewed self] which characterized your previous manner of life and becomes corrupt through lusts and desires that spring from delusion.
And be constantly renewed in the spirit of your mind [having a fresh mental and spiritual attitude],

*And put on the new nature (the regenerate self) created in
God's image,
[Godlike] in true righteousness and holiness.
Therefore, rejecting all falsity and being done now with it,
let everyone express the truth with his neighbor, for we are
all parts of one body and members of one another.*
Ephesians 4:21-25 The Amplified Bible

Studying and meditation on God's truth prepares you to change your thoughts and attitudes that are harmful to yourself and to others. Wearing that **belt of truth** enables you to renew your mindsets and practices so that you have the defense you need against the lies of the enemy. Your brain is actually transformed to think the thoughts of God and reflect His truth in your life.

Jesus Christ endured the cross, went to the pit of hell, and faced the enemy head-on to overcome all his evil ways and arise victorious to secure your salvation and defend you as a new creation. He now sits at the right hand of Father God to intervene on your behalf and defend you against those same evil ways of the enemy. Thus, you are protected from the effects of trauma and your defense is secured with the **helmet of salvation**.

SWORD OF THE SPIRIT

*...and the sword that the Spirit wields, which is the
Word of God.*
Ephesians 6:17b The Amplified Bible

A warrior going into battle clothed in strong armor would not be wise to proceed without a weapon. Yes, he needs protection from the weapons of the enemy, but he also needs a weapon of his own to pursue and defeat his enemy.

So, as a spiritual warrior, you need a powerful weapon as well. And that weapon is the **Word of God.** Every piece of your spiritual armor is created by acting on the Word of God in your life. His truth leads you to repentance which ushers you into salvation which equips you to live righteously and unafraid and teaches you how to hold your ground in battle.

But the Lord doesn't just want you to be dressed like a warrior, He wants you to actually fight like a warrior—His warrior! So, you need a mighty weapon to defeat your enemy. The **Word of God** is that weapon. How is the Word of God a tool for salvation but also a mighty weapon?

God's truth is strong and powerful and creative. He used His words to create the universe and all who occupy it. His words are life changing. He is the author of life itself.

Faith empowers us to see that the universe was created and beautifully coordinated by the power of God's words! He spoke and the invisible realm gave birth to all that is seen.
Hebrews 11:3 The Passion Translation

The enemy of your soul, the devil, is the one who brings death into your atmosphere. He desires to take the life that God created and blot it out forever. He wants to destroy all that God made good and bring it to an end.

God has a specific and unique plan for your life. He placed the ability and desire for that unique plan inside of you when He created you. He sent you into the Earth realm at just the right time for you to fulfill that plan and reflect His glorious design during your life. That plan develops and matures as you spend time in His presence, learning about Him and gaining His wisdom so you can appropriate His power to carry it out to the fullest.

The thief comes only in order to steal and kill and destroy.
I came that they may have and enjoy life, and have it in
abundance (to the full, till it overflows).
John 10:10 The Amplified Bible

The devil wants to keep you from fulfilling that plan and bringing glory to God on Earth. The enemy of your soul wants to keep you distracted, distraught, and discouraged so you are unable to fulfill the glorious design God has for your life.

So, you need a mighty weapon to push the enemy back and take the ground you are to influence and occupy. That mighty weapon is the **spoken Word of God.** Just as God created the world and all people with His words, you can create change and godly, influential power with your words that are inspired by the Lord.

As you gain knowledge of God's written words in the Bible, you can begin to declare those words in power as the Holy Spirit inspires you. The Holy Spirit is the powerful force behind the Word of God when He inspires you to pray and declare it **out loud.** Silent prayer is a valid communication between you and the Father. But spoken prayers based on God's Word carry valuable and powerful influence into the atmosphere around you. As Holy Spirit inspires you to pray or declare God's Word out loud, He then carries it into the place where it is needed for God's light to push away the darkness of the devil.

When Jesus Christ becomes your Savior and Lord, then you dwell in His holy light and carry it with you wherever you go in obedience to Him:

*In the beginning [before all-time] was the Word (Christ),
and the Word was with God, and the Word was God
Himself.*
He was present originally with God.
*All things were made and came into existence through
Him; and without Him was not even one thing made that
has come into being.*
In Him was Life, and the Life was the Light of men.
*And the Light shines on in the darkness, for the darkness
has never overpowered it*
*[put it out or absorbed it or appropriated it,
and is unreceptive to it].*
John 1:1-5 The Amplified Bible

Christ is the Living Word of God. He sits at the right hand of Father God interceding for you every day. So, as you study His words in the Bible and listen to His voice within your spirit, you will gain wisdom on how to speak His words into your life and the circumstances you are involved in. Then, as you pray and declare His word over your concerns, He will watch over His word to perform it. The light of Christ that is contained in those words will overpower the darkness that is present. His words, spoken through your mouth, will become like a mighty sword that scatters the enemy and reflects the light of Christ into the atmosphere.

This powerful **Sword of the Spirit** has two sides. Some swords have only one sharp side, but others have two sharp sides. God has provided us with a powerful sword with two sharp sides.

*For the Word that God speaks is alive and full of power
[making it active, operative, energizing, and effective]; it is
sharper than any two-edged sword, penetrating to the*

dividing line of the breath of life (soul) and [the immortal] spirit, and of joints and marrow [of the deepest parts of our nature], exposing and sifting and analyzing and judging the very thoughts and purposes of the heart.
Hebrews 4:12 The Amplified Bible

We have been looking at the side of our sword that represents the spoken Word of God and is inspired and reflected in His written scriptural words. The other side of this Sword of the Spirit was revealed in the book of Acts on the day of Pentecost. When Christ appeared to His disciples after His death and resurrection, He instructed them to wait in Jerusalem for the baptism of the Holy Spirit (Acts 1:3-5).

On the day of Pentecost, as the disciples were waiting, they were filled with the presence of the Holy Spirit and began to speak in unknown tongues (Acts 2:1-4). These tongues enabled them to speak in languages they had not ever learned and people from many other countries could understand what they were saying in the language of their own country. It was a miraculous demonstration of the spiritual language of God.

God speaks in every language ever known to man and He speaks a spiritual language that He has designed to influence the spiritual realm. Holy Spirit enables us to also speak God's language as we yield ourselves to His presence and power. These unknown tongues bypass our mental capabilities and help us pray prayers and declarations and even songs that only God can inspire and articulate.

So, unknown tongues declared in faith by the leadership of the Holy Spirit, is the other side of God's two-edged sword that He has made available to all believers in Christ. Praying in tongues is a powerful weapon against the powers of darkness. By praying in this spiritual language, we are allowing the Holy Spirit to pray the perfect will of God for a situation we are concerned about. And as we give this spiritual language a voice, we can be inspired and receive understanding we have not had before.

The Apostle Paul gave the Corinthian believers a wonderful understanding of the gift of speaking in tongues. He addresses the need for order and simplicity while praying in tongues within a church gathering. In 1 Corinthians 14, he explains what tongues are and how to use them to the best benefit of all who would hear them in a group setting.

First, he explains what speaking in tongues is:

For one who speaks in an [unknown] tongue speaks not to men but to God, for no one understands or catches his meaning, because in the [Holy] Spirit he utters secret truths and hidden things [not obvious to the understanding].
1 Corinthians 14:2 The Amplified Bible

When you pray in tongues, you are actually praying the very secrets of God Himself. You can pray beyond your present understanding of a situation. Praying in tongues gives you the ability to pray God's perfect will and desire for the circumstances you are concerned about. That is an amazing gift from our Father of Lights.

Paul encourages those who speak in tongues to ask God for the understanding of what they have said so that all who hear may be edified and gain an understanding of God's will and desire for their situation. He does not forbid it but encourages those who use this gift to seek understanding from the Lord so everyone may be enlightened with God's wisdom.

> *So it is with yourselves; since you are so eager and ambitious to possess spiritual endowments and manifestations of the [Holy] Spirit, [concentrate on] striving to excel and to abound [in them] in ways that will build up the church.*
> *Therefore, the person who speaks in an [unknown] tongue should pray [for the power] to interpret and explain what he says.*
> *For if I pray in an [unknown] tongue, my spirit [by the Holy Spirit within me] prays, but my mind is unproductive [it bears no fruit and helps nobody].*
> *Then what am I to do? I will pray with my spirit [by the Holy Spirit that is within me], but I will also pray [intelligently] with my mind and understanding; I will sing with my spirit [by the Holy Spirit that is within me], but I will sing [intelligently] with my mind and understanding also.*
> 1 Corinthians 14:12-15 The Amplified Bible

So, Paul is encouraging believers to pray in spiritual tongues as well as praying with their understanding. By praying in tongues, you give the Lord a way to stir up your spirit to say in your own language the things He wants you to pray into your atmosphere so that you and others may be edified and lifted up.

Did you catch the fact that you can sing in tongues as well? What a wonderful way to enter into the courts of the Lord in perfect worship and union with Holy Spirit! You can worship beyond your own understanding of who God is and how awesome He is. Then, as you seek Him in faith, He can bring to your mind words of wisdom and worship in your own language so that you and others can be inspired and encouraged.

Paul was truly grateful for being able to speak in tongues, but he also wanted the church to understand how to use this amazing gift in ways to benefit all who gathered to worship and pray.

I thank God that I speak in [strange] tongues (languages)
more than any of you or all of you put together;
Nevertheless, in public worship, I would rather say five
words with my understanding and intelligently in order to
instruct others, than ten thousand words in a [strange]
tongue (language).
1 Corinthians 14:18-19 The Amplified Bible

My personal experience with speaking in tongues as a form of intercession and spiritual warfare has been most encouraging and uplifting. If I am alone, I am free to pray in the spirit and with my understanding as the Holy Spirit leads. Many times, when I am praying over difficult situations, I will begin by worshipping and praying in tongues. Then, the Holy Spirit will bring scriptures to mind that speak God's will into that situation. He also inspires me to make declarations in my own language out loud so that I am encouraged and empowered to know that the Lord is working with me to change the circumstances for the benefit of those I am praying for.

If I am praying in a group of like-minded believers who also pray in tongues, then I feel free to pray both with my understanding as well as in the spiritual language the Lord provides. I do not do either to overpower another person's prayers but to complement what is being addressed in the group.

If I am praying with a group who may not speak in tongues, then I pray with my understanding and trust the Lord to inspire me to pray scriptural prayers that will bring His will and desire into that situation. My desire is to follow Holy Spirit to do what He wants to be done in either situation.

It is vital for you to declare His inspired words as often as He leads you to. A soldier doesn't drop his sword after the first swipe at the enemy. You must continue to declare His word until you see change. Don't drop your sword! Be persistent and faithful to speak His powerful words into the atmosphere and expect the authority they carry to change what He desires to change.

Waiting for change to manifest can be hard. So, you must also battle against despair, hopelessness, and fear by meditating on and declaring His words of promise, hope, and encouragement over yourself and the people in your realm of influence.

...And be not grieved and depressed, for the joy of the Lord is your strength and stronghold.
Nehemiah 8:10b The Amplified Bible

These words were spoken to the people of Israel after they heard the words of the Lord and were convicted of their sins against Him. They began to weep in repentance. But Nehemiah encouraged them to be joyful because now they knew what the Lord wanted them to understand about their lifestyles.

Joy does not always come easy amid difficult circumstances. But being joyful about the power of God and His ability to change things provides you strength to endure the wait and continue to battle in faith with His powerful weapon of war—**the Sword of the Spirit!** His word is eternal and all-powerful and can see you through to victory!

As you focus on our Almighty God in praise and worship, joy will come to your soul and strengthen you to keep using His powerful words as your sword to push back the enemy and defeat his plots and plans on the Earth. Your shield of faith will guard your heart so you can continue in joyful strength and abide in His mighty stronghold.

Now faith brings our hopes into reality and becomes the foundation needed to acquire the things we long for. It is all the evidence required to prove what is still unseen. This testimony of faith is what previous generations were commended for.
Hebrews 11:1-2 The Passion Translation

As you continue to use your mighty **sword of the spirit—the spoken Word of God,** you will actually affect the lives of the generations that will follow you. Think about that! Even if you do not see a change in your lifetime, as many of the saints of old experienced, the generations that follow you can benefit from your prayers and declarations of truth and faith. Your children and grandchildren can be encouraged and built up through those faith-filled words that you speak into the atmosphere.

As a mighty warrior in God's army, you have the power to change history and create a better future for those that follow you. What a glorious and precious assignment that is for you to fulfill!

CHAPTER 5
Wielding Your Sword

God's Word is our foremost weapon of warfare against the enemy of our souls. Remember God created the Earth with His **spoken** word. You cannot leave your sword in its sheath. You must take it out and swipe it at the enemy. So, speaking the Word of the Lord **out loud** is the way you wield your spiritual sword.

Making declarations based on scripture and led by the Holy Spirit is our powerful weapon against the forces of darkness operating in our world. God's word is eternal and unchanging. The enemy has no power to negate it or make it go away. Our silence is the way we become defeated in personal battles and in territorial battles. We must declare the truth over every circumstance as we learn of God's desire to change it.

As you read the Word of God, ask the Holy Spirit to highlight scriptures that He wants you to declare over yourself, your family, your community, and your nation. The Psalms contain many wonderful prayers and declarations that can be pronounced into our modern world to effect change and bring God's desire into the present. The New Testament is filled with prayers and encouraging words from Jesus, the apostles, and the prophets. You cannot go wrong quoting scriptures into your daily circumstances to encourage yourself and to defeat the onslaught of the enemy's lies and threats.

The following passages are examples of declarations and prayers I have prayed often for myself and others over the years. These are just a few examples that may help you in putting together your own powerful passages that can encourage you and defeat the enemy of your soul.

Personal prayer and declaration based on Psalm 103:1-5 The Amplified Bible:

BLESS the Lord, O my soul; and all that is [deepest] within me, bless His holy name!
Bless the Lord, O my soul, and forget not [one of] all His benefits—
Lord You forgive [every one of] all my iniquities,
You heal [each one of] all of my diseases,
You redeem my life from the pit and corruption,
You beautify, dignify, and crown me with loving-kindness and tender mercy;
You satisfy my mouth [my necessity and desire at my personal age and situation] with good so that my youth, renewed, is like the eagle's [strong, overcoming, soaring]! [Isa. 40:31.]
You Lord execute righteousness and justice [not for me only, but] for all who are oppressed.

A prayer I pray for our family based on Ephesians 1:17-21 The Amplified Bible:

Father God of our Lord Jesus Christ, Father of glory, grant me and my family wisdom and revelation [of insight into mysteries and secrets] in the [deep and intimate] knowledge of Yourself,
By having the eyes of our hearts flooded with light, so that we can know and understand the hope to which You have called us, and how rich is Your glorious inheritance in the saints (Your set-apart ones),
And [so that we can know and understand] what is the immeasurable and unlimited and surpassing greatness of

Your power in and for us who believe, as demonstrated in the working of Your mighty strength, which You exerted in Christ when You raised Him from the dead and seated Him at Your [own] right hand in the heavenly [places], far above all rule and authority and power and dominion and every name that is named, not only in this age and in this world, but also in the age and the world which is to come. May Your kingdom come and your will be done in my family for Your honor and glory. In Jesus name, Amen.

Recently, I did a prayer walk with a friend at a local school and made these declarations based on the desires I know the Lord has to make our public schools a safe and healthy haven for children, teachers, staff and parents. I encourage you to make these and other biblical declarations over the schools in your community.

Father we come before You today, in the Mighty name of Jesus Christ, on behalf of the State of _____ school system. We are believing and proclaiming Your will to be done and Your kingdom to come in the administrative staff, the teachers and the students that attend these schools.

We specifically lift up (school of your choice) for your protection over the staff, teachers and students.

We command the twisting of words and every evil agenda of the enemy to bow the knee to the truth of God's word and the desire of His heart for this school.

We command fear, anxiety, and confusion to come off of the administrative staff, the teachers, students and their parents.

We speak peace, joy, and the strategy of the Lord for the teachers, students and staff.

Lord, we are expecting an avalanche of Your life-giving change to come into this school system and the systems all over _____.

We declare the removal of all evil agendas and employees by Your hand of justice.

We declare that every evil file of intention or history about the School Board, administrators or teachers will be revealed, and justice will be carried out by Your angelic warriors according to Your divine direction.

We declare that the line is drawn that will forbid the indoctrination of children with wokeness, gender confusion, disrespect for the constitution of the United States of America and lies about the founding of this country.

We declare that every evil attempt to hurt, malign or destroy the lives of students, teachers and administrators will cease and have no power to be carried out anywhere in the State of _____ and across this nation.

We command every ungodly pressure and demand of performance from teachers and administrators to cease and all unnecessary requirements for reports and paperwork to cease and fall away.

We ask you Lord to make a way for these school systems to prioritize the healthy basic academic teachings for children and desist in trying to teach children principles that only parents have the right and responsibility to teach.

We declare life, liberty, and the pursuit of happiness over these school systems.

We declare that school hours, breaks and schedules will be designed for the healthy benefit of students, families, and teachers.

We call forth Your mighty angelic warriors to guard and preserve the lives of every staff member, teacher, and student as they travel to and from school and as they stay on school grounds.

We declare that no evil intruders will be able to touch or enter the property of the school buildings or buses.

We thank You Lord God Almighty that You make the schools in _____ and across the nation a safe haven for teachers, staff, students and parents!

The prayer and declarations below are written for the United States of America. If you are a citizen or supporter of our country, I urge you to pray and declare these things daily. If you live in another country, I pray they will serve as a guide for you to make righteous declarations over your own place of residence.

Father, God, thank You for creating the United States of America to be a nation founded on the principles found in Your Word. Our nation was created to be a lighthouse to other nations pointing them to the truth that Jesus Christ is our risen Savior and King. I make these declarations based on Your Word and our Constitution written to reflect Your desires for this nation.

I declare that Jesus is Lord over the United States of America.

I declare that You, Lord God, are restoring and reforming this nation to reflect Your glory and to protect and preserve those who will follow Your desires.

I declare that our government will only pass laws that are based on biblical principles and the original constitution of our nation.

I declare that all those in leadership who do not uphold the constitution and reflect Your desires will be removed from their places of influence.

I declare the USA will protect the innocent and seek justice for those who oppose life for the unborn.

I declare that our borders will be secured against criminals and all those who seek to bring harm to the citizens of the USA.

I declare that our schools will be a safe haven for students, teachers, administrators and parents.

I declare that our personal rights as parents will not be violated by any department of the government or agency of the educational system.

I declare that we will be free from the exploitation of our natural resources by those who seek to control them.

I declare an avalanche of righteous revival across this nation that will begin a dynamic outreach of hope, peace and love to other nations.

I declare that this nation was birthed by the Lord God Almighty for His honor and His glory,

I declare that the Righteous Judge of the Universe will bring justice to all who ignore and spurn our birthright as a nation unto God.

I declare that the unrighteous who plan evil against this nation will fall into their own traps and be held accountable for their deeds of injustice.

I declare the roar of the Lion of Judah over the United States of America and America will be saved and healed to reflect Almighty God's original plan for this nation.

Thank You Father, Son, and Holy Spirit for having mercy on us as a nation and gracing us to rise up to honor and glorify You as Lord and King. In the mighty name of Jesus!

CHAPTER 6
Preparing to Move Forward in Battle

My prayer for you is that every moment you will experience the measureless power of God made available to you through faith. Then your lives will be an advertisement of this immense power as it works through you!
This is the explosive and mighty resurrection power that was released when God raised Christ from the dead and exalted him to the place of highest honor and supreme authority in the heavenly realm!
And now he is exalted higher than all the thrones and principalities, above every ruler and authority, and above every realm of power there is. He is gloriously enthroned over every name that is ever praised, not only in this age, but in the age that is coming!
Ephesians 1:19-21 The Passion Translation

Soldiers do not become warriors overnight. They must go through extensive training to learn how to wear their armor properly and use their weapons proficiently. As a soldier in God's army, you must also train and practice how to use your sword—the Word of the Lord—with wisdom and accuracy. And you must always make sure your armor is in place to protect you from the onslaught of the enemy.

Our Father God wants us to be ready to go into battle at any moment. Sometimes we will be defending the ground we hold and sometimes we will be moving forward to take more ground for the Kingdom of God. In either case, we need to be alert and confident in the call of God upon our lives.

I believe God is always training us for MORE! He is infinite in power and majesty and mercy. As we continue to seek Him and explore His Word, He will move us forward into higher places of power, authority, and purpose. The goal is to know Him deeply and intimately and to share His desires and plans. Without study and prayer, we will not be able to hold our own personal ground or begin to take more ground for His Kingdom on Earth.

We all spend years in education and training to be able to earn a living and gain the things we desire to make our lives and families comfortable and protected. So, as a child of God and a soldier in His army, we must spend time and energy studying His Word that directs our steps and teaches us about our God and ourselves. That is the only way we can expect to grow in faith and fulfill our purpose in life.

Keep your heart focused on the Lord every day. Always seek His counsel to direct your steps and form the words of influence He wants you to speak. Every day is a new opportunity to be a powerful representative of the love, mercy, wisdom, and power of Almighty God. He will not disappoint as you move forward in faith and obedience.

A soldier must go through many steps of preparation before they enter a battle. In the previous chapters, you can see the progression of training necessary to become a warrior in the Kingdom of God.

First, you must understand the Lord is the ultimate authority over all creation. He has chosen to share that authority with all those who believe He is God Almighty, and that Jesus Christ is their Savior and Lord. And Holy Spirit has been given to believers as their equipping and comforting assistant.

Secondly, you must know who the enemy is. Our enemy is satan and all his fallen angels of deception. They use people to perform their works of darkness through deception and oppression.

Thirdly, you must learn about your armor and how to wear it properly and effectively. That knowledge comes from and is founded on the Living Word of God as recorded in the written Word of God.

Finally, you must learn how to use your mighty weapon, the spoken Word of God, with accuracy and power through the prayers you pray and the declarations you make out loud into the earthly realm.

But before a soldier goes into battle, the most important thing he must do is prepare his heart for the fight. In the natural, a soldier must realize he may face death. There is no way for him to know if he will survive the act of war. It is dangerous and unpredictable. So, he must prepare to give his all—even in the face of death.

As a spiritual warrior, you must be prepared to face the enemy knowing that God is your Creator, Savior, and Lord. You must be willing to obey His instructions and face the enemy with God's truth and righteous acts. Your heart must be free from doubt, fear, and sin. You cannot face the enemy if you are agreeing with his deceptions and lies and evil desires.

Jesus was fully prepared to face the enemy as He began His journey to the cross. Yes, He is the Lord, but He was and is fully a man. He experienced the same temptations and fears that you or I have ever faced. But He knew who He was and that He was following the Father's righteous and wise directions.

These are the comforting and powerful words of Jesus as He addressed His disciples before He was crucified:

Peace I leave with you; My [own] peace I now give and bequeath to you. Not as the world gives do I give to you. Do not let your hearts be troubled, neither let them be afraid. [Stop allowing yourselves to be agitated and disturbed; and do not permit yourselves to be fearful and intimidated and cowardly and unsettled.]

You heard Me tell you, I am going away and I am coming [back] to you. If you [really] loved Me, you would have been glad, because I am going to the Father; for the Father is greater and mightier than I am.

And now I have told you [this] before it occurs, so that when it does take place you may believe and have faith in and rely on Me.

I will not talk with you much more, for the prince (evil genius, ruler) of the world is coming. And he has no claim on Me. [He has nothing in common with Me; there is nothing in Me that belongs to him, and he has no power over Me.]

But [Satan is coming and] I do as the Father has commanded Me, so that the world may know (be convinced) that I love the Father and that I do only what the Father has instructed Me to do. [I act in full agreement with His orders.] Rise, let us go away from here.

John 14:27-31 The Amplified Bible

The first thing Jesus did was to give the peace He was experiencing to His disciples. He was at peace even though He knew what horrors He would face. He instructed them not to let fear and intimidation take over their thoughts. Then, He gave them hope of His coming again so they could be glad even though He was leaving. He was leaving them a hopeful picture so they could continue in faith to follow His lead after He was gone.

His final words in this passage speak of His position before the enemy (satan). Jesus knew who He was, the Son of God Almighty. He also knew that He was obeying the Father's desire because of His great love for Him. Jesus was in complete agreement with the Father's plan for the salvation of mankind, even though He would have to go to the cross and engage the enemy in the pit of hell. He had no doubt that the Father's plan would succeed, and He would rise again to join Him in the throne room of Heaven.

Because Jesus was in obedience to the Father, He knew that satan could not defeat Him. Jesus had no sin that would make Himself vulnerable to the enemy's assault. Jesus had nothing in common with the devil. His heart was fully prepared for the horrendous battle He was facing. He knew He would be victorious even in the face of torture and death. The heart of Jesus was pure and clean before the Father and it prepared Him for the battle of all battles on Earth and in Heaven.

We must also prepare our hearts for battle before we face the enemy of our souls. We must be sure our attitude and desire are to please the Lord and obey His instructions—even if it means we will have to die to our own plans or desires.

Our focus must be to know that we are free from sin through the blood of Jesus and to keep our hearts clean by being honest and humble before the Lord. He knows our every motive and desire. We cannot hide from His view, but we can be at peace if we are honest and repentant when we experience sinful thoughts or actions. We cannot have anything in common with the enemy of our souls if we are to be victorious on the battlefield.

This charge and admonition I commit in trust to you, Timothy, my son, in accordance with prophetic intimations

which I formerly received concerning you, so that inspired and aided by them you may wage the good warfare, Holding fast to faith (that leaning of the entire human personality on God in absolute trust and confidence) and having a good (clear) conscience. By rejecting and thrusting from them [their conscience], some individuals have made shipwreck of their faith.
1 Timothy 1:18-19 The Amplified Bible

This is the advice that the Apostle Paul gave to his young friend, Timothy, who was to oversee the body of believers in Ephesus. He was encouraging Timothy to hold onto the prophetic pictures that Paul had of Timothy as a leader in the Body of Christ. He knew this young man needed a clear picture of his responsibilities and his ability to lead and wage war against the enemy of his own soul.

Paul also reminded Timothy that he must put his entire trust in the Lord to remain pure and keep his heart clean before the Lord. Faith in the Lord and His wisdom for living on Earth was the only way he could keep his conscience clean and free from sin.

True faith comes with a desire and determination to live honestly before the Lord, otherwise, one cannot remain on the course the Lord has created them to follow as His representative. A clear conscience and a pure, honest heart before the Lord enable us to press into the battles we face in life. When you know you are living in agreement with the Lord concerning attitudes and actions, you are prepared to use the Word of the Lord confidently and accurately as He instructs you to face the enemy and cut off his evil plans.

You cannot use the Word of the Lord as a weapon against the enemy if you are not living by the Word of the Lord. **Jesus is the Living Word.** He rules and reigns from the throne room of Heaven through the prayers and declarations of those who follow Him in truth and purity. **Jesus is *the Way, the Truth, and the Life*!** (John 14:6) Jesus is our example of a victorious, powerful warrior who defeated His enemy in the enemy's own domain (hell).

The following passage from Paul's prayer in the book of Ephesians explains our position in Christ as warriors with great power:

And [so that you can know and understand] what is the immeasurable and unlimited and surpassing greatness of His power in and for us who believe, as demonstrated in the working of His mighty strength,
Which He exerted in Christ when He raised Him from the dead and seated Him at His [own] right hand in the heavenly [places],
Far above all rule and authority and power and dominion and every name that is named [above every title that can be conferred], not only in this age and in this world, but also in the age and the world which are to come.
And He has put all things under His feet and has appointed Him the universal and supreme Head of the church [a headship exercised throughout the church], [Ps. 8:6.]
Which is His body, the fullness of Him Who fills all in all [for in that body lives the full measure of Him Who makes everything complete,
and Who fills everything everywhere with Himself].
Ephesians 1:19-23 The Amplified Bible
(Emphasis is mine)

The Father has made Jesus the Head of the church. The church is those who have believed Jesus is their Savior and Lord and follow His lead. The body cannot operate in fullness and power without being vitally connected to the head who sends out the signals needed to operate at full capacity. As explained in this passage, Jesus has full rule and authority and dominion over every other power ever created! If you are connected to the Head in a true, intimate, and pure relationship, you have the power and authority to carry out His plans and purposes on Earth.

Sin separates the Body from the Head. Repentance and obedience restore that connection and the Body can function at the highest level as instructed by the Lord. Preparing your heart before the Lord through honesty and repentance gives you all you need to go into battle with the Living Word as your protection and power to defeat the enemy of God Himself.

The following scripture is a great description of life without Jesus compared to a pure life in a relationship with Him:

I know you are embarrassed now about the things you used to do with your body; I mean was it worth it? What reward or return did you get but spiritual death? Sin is a cul-de-sac.
Consider your life now; there are no outstanding debts; you owe sin nothing! A life bonded to God yields the sacred expression of his character and completes in your experience what life was always meant to be.
The reward of the law is death, the gift of grace is life! The bottom line is this:
sin employs you like a soldier for its cause and rewards you with death; God gifts you with the highest quality of life all wrapped in Christ Jesus our Leader.
Romans 6:21-13 The Mirror Bible

There is no greater gift to you than knowing that you are in an unbroken relationship with Father, Son, and Holy Spirit. Sin is the only thing that can separate you from that life-giving relationship with Almighty God. You were born to be a warrior in God's army not a soldier in the devil's army. Repentance from sin and obedience to the Lord's direction for your life keeps that vital relationship active and powerful as you face the battles you encounter on this Earth.

Then, you are always ready for any challenge or battle you might have to face. You are also ready to actively confront the enemy and push him out of your territory through prayer and declaration of God's words.

Holy Spirit is present with you to convict you of sin and equip you to go in the right direction to fulfill the divine purpose God has created for you. Your Father loves you as His child. Jesus loves you as His sibling. Holy Spirit loves you like a nurturing mother. You are a part of the Body of Christ. As an **active** member of the Body of Christ, repentance and obedience to the Holy Spirit prepare you to be a successful and powerful warrior in the Kingdom of God.

Step by step, Holy Spirit will counsel you and teach you how to be a successful and productive citizen of the Kingdom of God and a responsible representative of His Kingdom on Earth. You are destined to change the world you live in. And the Lord has many ways for you to influence and assist those around you in becoming the people God created them to be.

Go forth and rejoice as you continue to grow stronger and more secure in your place in the family of God and the army of the King of kings!

You were born to be His warrior!

ABOUT THE AUTHOR

Angela Brown is a student and lover of the Word of God. She loves interceding in prayer and sharing her faith through writing and speaking. She is the author of a study book of Psalm 110, *His Footstool: The Door to Your Destiny,* and three devotionals: *Secrets from the Sanctuary, I AM, who am I?* and *A Word for All Seasons,* a yearlong devotional.

Angela has written articles for periodicals and assisted other authors in compiling and writing their own publications. She is an active intercessor and enjoys teaching the Word of God and encouraging others to thrive in their creative giftings.

Angela and her husband, Jackie, have been married for 55 years and reside in Marietta, Georgia close to their children, grandchildren, and great-grandchildren.

Angela's books are available through Amazon, or you can contact her at awbrown1@bellsouth.net.

Made in the USA
Columbia, SC
12 March 2024